The
Dinosaur
Drawing
Delivery

by Conor McIntyre
illustrated by Judith Rossell

Harcourt
SCHOOL PUBLISHERS

Printed in Mexico

ISBN 10: 0-15-351421-3
ISBN 13: 978-0-15-351421-0

Ordering Options
ISBN 10: 0-15-351212-1 (Grade 2 Advanced Collection)
ISBN 13: 978-0-15-351212-4 (Grade 2 Advanced Collection)
ISBN 10: 0-15-358056-9 (package of 5)
ISBN 13: 978-0-15-358056-7 (package of 5)

2 3 4 5 6 7 8 9 10   050   15 14 13 12 11 10 09 08 07

"That dinosaur you've drawn looks tough, Lily," said Mr. Allen, Lily's teacher.

" I know," said Lily. "I gave him gigantic shoes to wear to make him look funny."

"Excellent!" said Mr. Allen. "All the drawings for the school art exhibit tomorrow look fantastic."

"It's time to go home now," said Mr. Allen. "Please leave your drawings on the shelf above the crayons, and don't forget to wash your hands."

Lily didn't want to leave her picture at school. She wanted to take it home to show her mom because her mom couldn't make it to the art exhibit tomorrow.

Lily carefully slipped her picture into her backpack. She would take it home to show her mom and then bring it back tomorrow.

That night, Lily proudly showed
her mom her dinosaur picture.

"What a great drawing!" said
Mom with interest. "I'm sorry
I can't attend the exhibit, but at least
I got to view your picture."

At school the next morning,
Mr. Allen said, "There's still work to
be done for the art exhibit. Please
get your pictures from the shelf, and
bring them to the display area."

Lily searched in her backpack
for her picture, but where was it?
Suddenly, she remembered that
she had left it on the edge of her
bed. She was going to put it in her
backpack last. Then, in her rush to
leave, she forgot it.

Suddenly, Lily saw Mom at the classroom door. She was holding up Lily's picture!

"You forgot your drawing, Lily," said Mom. "You left it at home."

Mr. Allen looked surprised. "I thought I asked you to put your picture on the shelf, Lily," he said.

"Is that true, Lily?" asked Mom.

Lily nodded. "I wanted to show you my picture," she said. "I know that you can't come to the art exhibit this afternoon. I'm really sorry I didn't listen, Mr. Allen."

"That's okay, Lily," said Mr. Allen, "but I wish you had asked me first. I would have understood."

That afternoon, the colorful
pictures went on display.
"Well done, Lily," said Mr. Allen.
"Your picture looks great."

"Is that your dinosaur, young lady?" asked a woman from the newspaper.

"It sure is," said Lily.

"May I take a photo of your picture for my article on the art exhibit?" asked the woman.

"You bet!" exclaimed Lily, with a big smile. Now her mom would get to see her dinosaur drawing in the newspaper, too!

14

Think Critically

1. What did Mr. Allen ask the children to do with their drawings?

2. How did Mr. Allen discover Lily had not put her drawing on the shelf?

3. How do you think Lily felt when Mom arrived at school with her drawing?

4. What are two things about this book that tell you it is fiction?

5. Do you think Lily made a good choice when she took her drawing home?

 **Social Studies**

Write a Paragraph   Write a paragraph about why Lily should have listened to Mr. Allen and why rules at school are important.

School-Home Connection Think of a time when you left something important at home or at school. Tell a family member about what happened and how you felt.